FIRST RAIN IN PARADISE

Gwyneth Lewis was Wales's National Poet from 2005 to 2006, the first writer to be given the Welsh laureateship. Her first six books of poetry in Welsh and English were followed by *Chaotic Angels* (2005) from Bloodaxe, which brought together the poems from her English collections, *Parables & Faxes*, *Zero Gravity* and *Keeping Mum*, and by *A Hospital Odyssey* (2010), and *Sparrow Tree* (2011), winner of the Roland Mathias Poetry Award (Wales Book of the Year) in 2012. Her sixth collection in English, *First Rain in Paradise*, was published by Bloodaxe in 2025.

Her other books include *Sunbathing in the Rain: A Cheerful Book about Depression* (Flamingo, 2002), *Two in a Boat: A Marital Voyage* (Fourth Estate, 2005), *The Meat Tree: new stories from the Mabinogion* (Seren, 2010), *Nightshade Mother: A Disentangling* (University of Wales Press, 2024) and *The Poetry Detective: Writing and Reading Poetry Through Fear* (Princeton University Press, 2025). With Rowan Williams she translated *The Book of Taliesin* (2019) for Penguin Classics. *Zero Gravity* won the Welsh Arts Council's Book of the Year in 1999 and her collection in Welsh, *Y Llofrudd Iaith* the same prize the following year. Both *Zero Gravity* and *Keeping Mum* were Poetry Book Society Recommendations.

Gwyneth Lewis composed the words on the front of the Wales Millennium Centre in Cardiff, opened in 2004. In 2014 she dramatised her book-length poem *A Hospital Odyssey* for the BBC, broadcast on Radio 4's *Afternoon Drama*, and delivered her Newcastle/Bloodaxe Poetry Lectures, published in *Quantum Poetics* (Bloodaxe Books, 2015).

She lives in Cardiff and teaches regularly for Middlebury College's Bread Loaf School of English in the US. She was Artist in Residence at Balliol College, Oxford, in 2023-25; she did her doctorate there and was elected an Honorary Fellow. She received a Cholmondeley Award in 2010 for a distinguished body of writing, and in 2022 she was awarded an MBE for her services to literature and mental health.

GWYNETH LEWIS

FIRST RAIN IN PARADISE

Copyright © Gwyneth Lewis 2025

ISBN: 978 1 78037 733 9

First published 2025 by
Bloodaxe Books Ltd,
Eastburn,
South Park,
Hexham,
Northumberland NE46 1BS.

www.bloodaxebooks.com
For further information about Bloodaxe titles
please visit our website and join our mailing list
or write to the above address for a catalogue.

LEGAL NOTICE

All rights reserved. No part of this book may be
reproduced, stored in a retrieval system, or
transmitted in any form, or by any means, electronic,
mechanical, photocopying, recording or otherwise,
without prior written permission from Bloodaxe Books Ltd.

Requests to publish work from this book
must be sent to Bloodaxe Books Ltd.

Gwyneth Lewis has asserted her right under
Section 77 of the Copyright, Designs and Patents Act 1988
to be identified as the author of this work.

Cover design: Neil Astley & Pamela Robertson-Pearce.

Printed in Great Britain by Bell & Bain Limited, 303 Burnfield Road,
Thornliebank, Glasgow G46 7UQ, Scotland, on acid-free paper
sourced from mills with FSC chain of custody certification.

Though you have done nothing shameful,
they will want you to be ashamed.
They will want you to kneel and weep
and say you should have been like them.

WENDELL BERRY
'Do Not Be Ashamed'

CONTENTS

I FALLING

Spiderings

15 Spider Mother
16 Snare
17 Maze
18 Missing
19 Not My Doll But Just Like Her
20 Any Eight Legs Will Do
21 Spidering
22 Away!

        ⊶✠⊷

25 Principalities, Dominions
26 Stage Manager's Notes
27 Helpless

II UNWELL

31 Auras

        ⊶✠⊷

34 Another Day Ill in Bed
35 Red Waistcoat
36 Will I?
37 Too Far
38 Persephone in CERN
39 Damage
40 Lips
41 Earrings from the Anti-Matter Factory
42 Under
43 Rogue Female
44 Fooled Me for Years with the Wrong Pronoun
45 Fallen Objects that Can't Be Saved

46 Relic
47 Chronic Fatigue
48 Desolation
49 Ice Mummy
50 The Long Crawl up Humanity's Beach
51 Ear, Nose and Throat
52 Grottarossa Mummy

III RECOVERY

55 Awake
56 *Flowers of the Wayside and Meadow*
57 A Litter Herbal
58 Late Blackberries
59 On Stopping the Anti-Depressants
60 Three Ways into Water
61 The Beat
62 Riverlarking

First Rain in Paradise

65 Previous
66 Shame
67 Kidnapped
68 Floods
69 Expulsion

71 Ornithology
72 An Explanation of Doily

77 NOTES & ACKNOWLEDGEMENTS

I **FALLING**

There is no relationship more narcissistic, as Freud himself remarks, than the relationship between mothers and their children… The first intimacy is an intimacy with a process of becoming, not with a person.

BERNARD WILLIAMS
Shame and Necessity

SPIDERINGS

Spider Mother

In that top corner, my torch picks out
the eight red eyes of one cunning spider,

wedged like a camera in its nest of wires.
I am the mote in each eye. Her gazes

trap me, like weighted nets
which have floored me more times

than I care to admit. Once I'm felled,
down she abseils and crawls

tickling, inside my ear, to lay eggs
into my brain. Those cells adjust

to their guest with seasons of migraine
through which I rest, until she emerges,

triumphant, through the arch of my mouth,
clad in chainmail of living armour:

glittering spiderlings, hatched from my mind –
if that can be called my own now, or home.

Snare

I won't call her spider,
                         though I do.
I live in the cage of her legs.
                         I've speared
my heart on a pointed stick to attract
                         carnivorous angels
which make a great racket of wings
                         but can't save.
'It's easy to leave, what stops you?',
                         others ask, baffled.
It's the snare in the brain, spring-loaded
                         for suicide. The knots
throb, electric, the anguish swells
                         till the trigeminal
nerve slithers out – a hot, pulsing snake –
                         through my eyeball,
leaving a spider's web tattooed
                         on my face
like a shattered windscreen.
                         This pattern alarms
employers but, honest, though I tell
                         of such horrors,
underneath, I'm a bit of a sweetie.

Maze

First, locate your original wound.
I come to in the bathroom, a body beside
me. Did we? Could I have? Check between legs
for dampness. Next, torso. Is this
my own blood? If not, then whose?

Tied to my hand is a thread of scarlet,
an electric cable zinging. Lose it, I die. So I follow
its pull through this house and its generations,
a crazed enfilade of dead ends, cluttered box rooms
while outside– huge thud, a gull

flies into a window. The bird is shattered
in three: the flesh slides down but its shadow
veers off at an angle, climbs, clicking sun's shutter
right in my face, the third is a burglar alarm
wailing, 'Emergency!'. Which one should I follow?

Missing

So, did I give my luck away? For piano
exams and degrees I wore a chain
with a silver spider plucking death
like a tune on her web, but in my favour.
I passed – how fortunate! My mam
'kept it safe', but now I can't find it.

No sign in the shoebox filled with Whitby jet
in tissue paper, moss agate brooches and –
swift recoil – underneath, a foetus mother
made from my nerves, nourished by ichor,
sour as wasp soup. She mewls for attention.
Too late. On me, her charm's broken.

I'll knit my own token instead: fling a cable
woven from habits of mind, the skill
of not-being-me flung over the chasm.
Once fast, I'll test the tension,
step out, eyes fixed on the other side,
to dance its wide road, with my parasol.

Not My Doll, But Just Like Her

I never loved mine, Siwan Elin: I opened
her clock face, its movement clogged dead,
seized up with dried spiders. She told
the wrong time because we were trapped
in rooms snowed under by dead-skin blizzards.

Round here skips mark the implacable massacre
of parents, each one a Pompeii. A hand sticks out
in appeal from a luggage landslide, I rescue a blonde
dolly: hand-knitted pinafore in sage, matching
knickers and vest. Who says you can't choose

your own household gods? In the past
my lares protector had been repaired
with elastic, holding head, torso, limbs
together. That perished, she fell apart,
so I'm forced to dispose of more body parts.

Any Eight Legs Will Do

I order a dress online: the design
is a blazon of giant arachnids, rampant –
emblems of terror tamed into fashion.
The Chinese wove spider threads
into luxury fabric, but gossamer,
like metaphor, tears.

The man who hands over my dress
has a forearm tattoo: a four-masted schooner –
full press of sails – attacked by Kraken.
The rigging frays, sailors fall
from shrouds into roiling
water, strakes part like lace –
and DOWN
goes the ship,
me with her,
mutating…

jellyfish brush past my leg,
light as lost breath…
tentacles twine, suckers
taste nipples, vulva…
we sink together…
I'm calm in my
monster's arms…

one flesh, we flush
iridescent with dreams
and I'm coming
undone
at the
seams

Spidering

Now for the mind-blinding fall
through thin air, the hissing spool
of silk high above me, a rope
that could hang me. I've anchored my web,

so pay out a loop, repeat, to form
a billowing compass rose
then listen, intently through outspread feet
for something to fall. Queen Jezebel

was flung by eunuchs from the palace window
onto the flagstones below, trampled
by horses, dog-savaged, till all that was left
were her palms, soles and skull.

Next I perceive the queen's physical rhyme:
a run-over vole on a lane, left pawpads
still perfect, held up in vain to deflect the tyre,
her torso crushed to a hand-pressed flower

of fur, exquisite. Then, something between
the two, I haul myself in. I neither survived
King Jehu's triumph nor the juggernaut wheel but –
don't ask me how, I'm still feeling, pulling.

Away!

A decade ago, I fell down a crevasse
and froze while, overhead passed

climbers in thousands on rickety ladders
chatting, making less sense than the stars.

Beneath them, my frost-bitten heart was their anchor,
though they didn't know it. Now sherpas

have found me. They resemble their fathers,
but taller and lead me gently to unfurl

my prayer-flags, lifting my arms in thanks,
but I've lived so long now on so little

that the merest wisp of a thermal
pulls me aloft, the stitch that was dropped

picked up again. I'm not alone:
around me are thousands ballooning

and, glinting from each self-suffering chain,
the star of a spider diamond.

Principalities, Domininons

I copy a Chalcid Wasp from a diagram,
admire, it, an insect cherubim,

four wings and forelegs all raised in praise,
as if grace falls like rain in this paper's grain.

'Holy! Holy! Holy!' Evangelical, it sings,
and I take care of the scimitar sting

of adrenaline over my heart. It feeds on flies,
spiders and ticks, which it keeps alive

while gorging. So, am I eaten or eater? Important
to know. I'm neither and both – for 'Providence…

keep[s] every animal in check by some other…more
powerful' (see Overleaf). Do you dare turn over?

Stage Manager's Notes

Clytemnestra awaits Agamemnon's return.
Move Towers to stage, rig pulleys. Lunch.
Fix lever in floor, chains to Stage Right.
Sound Quiet Time...   Call ends.

Cast fit-up. Cassandra's shoes
too tight. Requires size 5.
Electra's boots fit ok. Cast out
of costume. Lunch. Chat with publicity. Tea.

One more person needed to catch Miss Blythe
as Iphigenia when she falls
into the trap. Scene six will require
a bowl. Knives have been ordered.

Gravy granules, mint, cochineal
is our stage blood recipe. Miss Blythe as Electra
fumbled her clingfilm, the illusory cut
on her hand didn't work, so she did it for real,

what a professional! Press night:
exit doors chained, as I can't control
those Furies. One phone went off, soon
stopped. Small audience, play well received:

Man in G6 is Stage 4 and she in A12
won't survive a collision. Bodies fall
into hot nets of blood. Long delay for curtain
call, unavoidable. No, no further notes for today.

Helpless

The tide at Castell Bach has tied
a noose to a cleft in the rock. I've tried
to dislodge it, but it was wedged hard
by muscles stronger than mine. The sea

hangs herself twice a day then revives,
like the wife in Solaris, only to die again
in pain – such cruel, pointless resurrections.

II UNWELL

The mother in early infancy is less significant and identifiable as an object than as a process that is identified with cumulative internal and external transformations.

CHRISTOPHER BOLLAS
The Shadow of the Object

Auras

Someone has strung fine aura beads,
using a needle and white-hot wire, tugged
through my optic nerve, to make
a pulsating necklace. Light rides
the Big Bang towards me, wielding a knife
of cauterising pain, its blade
one photon wide, precise.

*   *   *

Ninth migraine this month. In my cave
I cower from noon's brain-piercing light.

I'm Eve, cover my face to blot
out the angel's laser sword. But I've seen
such sights.

*   *   *

That rogue, Robert Graves, located
the floating islands of Celtic legend
in the migrainous brain. Are they privileged visions?
Atlantis explodes. Is that flash
in the visual cortex an Avalon?
No, brain malfunction.

*   *   *

Turn the world down, it hurts. Route 125
runs through my cranium. A Harley purrs
ten miles away; huge trucks roar,
bear down on me from the Gap. I'm roadkill,
waiting for the coup de grâce.

* * *

A windless wood. Greenery strobes,
shade jazzes. That leaf
is rowing a private breeze, anomalous. There!
Can't you see it? Oh, super-
sensitive
me.

* * *

Ice Halo™

Wearable Ice Pack for Migraine!

Put it on front to back. Fasten hook and loop...
Fuggeddit. Can't even see. I'm a blur in the mirror:
A man in a turban, William Cowper, poor soul,
Before he went mad. *Is that kohl
round your eyes?* No, pain. It's my Bedouin
look. *And the yashmak?* For the coming storm
of ground glass, each sliver
a prism of flaying sun.

* * *

Are those mice in the rafters, or a fountain pen
scratching on paper? In the dark come the visiting dead:
William Blake, under angels' command, complains
That words skitter away, like electrical termites.

Give me moths for eyelids, or a world
I can bear. Please stop now, I'm tired, no
please carry on

*　*　*

Migraine nineteen. Eyes covered, I play
Blindman's Buff, guess at the world. That's Suzanne
taking the puppy out; that's the bin man's buggy and that,
Ladies and Gentlemen, is the Hermit Thrush,
master blacksmith at her forge, unmaking
the chainmail that covers her breast, link
by unbearably heavy link. And failing.

*　*　*

With the next aura – before pain arrives –
will you drive me over the Gap, up the Mad
River Valley, to the Bobbin Mill falls?
Lead me to a shaded pool
before sun warms it, push me in, so I rise
into the white-lace mantilla cascade,
comforted, for a few moments, with cold.

Another Day Ill in Bed

I've been slain, like hay
in the second cut and laid
on my bed. Two fields away
the illness machine

roars murder. I hear
my mind's creatures whisper:
'Buzzard and crow turn overhead
already! Run, for God's sake,

while you can, for the hedges'
shelter! In a moment, a tractor
will return with the baler
to start in earnest on the harvest.'

Red Waistcoat

A ewe has unbuttoned her woollen coat
along her sternum to display the scarlet

lining. Inside, her organs are pinned,
hot watches. Magpies have seized her eyes

to try out her gaze. It's a social occasion: kites,
buzzards and crow companions – anatomy students all –

fall into raked seating for Dr Tulp's
dissection at the Guild of Surgeons,

each detail revealed; they especially crave
fat's amber beads, still warm on her person.

Will I?

The herb called *Will I Ever Feel
Better?* is to be used
only to treat the gravest wounds

that must – despite the patient's protests –
be kept open, so they can heal
from the inside out. Summer comes, summer

goes. So little recovery. Being alive
is both trauma and sovereign
remedy. You cannot choose.

Too Far

I'm watching birds,
but see my mind

unfurl. Origami
time refolds,

then pleats this thrush
to a decoration

on a Christmas cake.
Press its prongs through

the Antarctic sheet
of icing to marzipan

permafrost, do it hard,
like so! I'm frozen, our ponies

are dead, pemmican
low, next depot

two days   at least
to go

Persephone at CERN

>'Look at me, Mother!
>I'm pirouetting
>on a beam one
>ion wide, en
>pointe!'

I tumble, past
death but not beyond
danger, dragged
from below, my flowers
scattered patterns
in a bubble chamber.

She finds me under the gravity waves
of winter. I'm sticky
with sex, hair tangled, irises
black from swallowing
six seeds of death,
so she bails me.

I beg her to lock me in
so I can't return
to that nightspot, disgrace
but always, always, I
find ways to escape.

Damage

Go on, ask me anything: for you
I'd walk to Moscow and back
without shoes, lick a toilet
clean, give you my teeth, hair
and health, or drink sick from a bowl,
like a saint living a point about love.

You say, 'Be well
and happy!' Oh no,
don't ask me for
that. Anything else
I could do, but not
that.

Lips

All night I was kissing Dylan and Huw,
his older brother. It was languorous,
luscious with silent vowels, occasional
teeth! Eloquent ritual of tongues:
slugs winding, sensuous in glair, leaving
lips chapped, beard rash, ecstatic bruises
strung, like gems, along my jawbone.

Such mutual longing! As when words rise
deep from the cave of breath,
resurgent: a stray bird in the house – bad luck! –
to be caught and flung out. Or subtle flutter
in the womb of mouth. How else redeem
myself from this dumbness? Be
darkness.   Wait.   Suffer.

Earrings from the Anti-Matter Factory

Which shall I choose? A ring of 'layered time'?
or 'corset, its strings undone'?
Sexy, but. 'Dark pearl in a storm'?
No, drop earrings: two isinglass panes

formed in the furnace by an angel's roar,
held in three silver rings, hooks cool
in my flesh. See the mica glitter
when I turn my head? Even better's that tug

from the drops as each pendulum tickles
my neck, glittering, kissing the flesh,
whispering secrets about inertia: how even
mighty mass longs for matter.

Under
(In memory of four killed in the 2011 Gleision drift-mine disaster)

Tops of trees, their roots in seams
of dark. King is under his mountain.

The cave's an open mouth whose words
are men who work their mountain.

Pine, larch and oak. Don't touch the bell
that tolls from out the mountain

or he will stir, and miners die
like light inside a mountain.

His breath is black and marks each face
that seeks beneath the mountain.

Leaves drift down, but they won't heal
the sentence of the mountain.

It's time to lose all hope and seal
the grave. The king's reclaimed his mountain.

Rogue Female

'It's me or you. I have prepared
with tireless discipline, and feats
of the bladder unusual in women
for your approach. Right now
a catapult with a fountain-pen bolt
is trained on your eye which, I see
from your fear, is a distinctive
green. This nib, filed fine,
will enter your brain. If you haven't
been hunting me, you won't be hurt
by my words. Move slowly now…
much depends on your answer.'

Fooled Me for Years with the Wrong Pronoun

You made me cry in cruel stations,
so I missed many trains. You married others
in plausible buildings. The subsequent son
became my boss. You promised me nothing
but blamed me for doubting when – who wouldn't?
If I knew how to please you – who have found
out my faults. In dreams I'm wild with guilt. Have pity,
kill it. Then, when I've lost all hope,
kiss me again, your mouth so supple –
I'd give anything for one more night –
that I go without thought. No, don't bite
or mark me. My husband already knows
exactly what owns me.

Fallen Objects that Can't Be Saved

The first was Satan, whose charisma
streaked through the heavens, a comet, and dropped –
according to Dante – to the bottom of hell,
where he's held in a glacier, refusing to change.
That's damnation. No river can rise from him, who refuses
to weep, consumes others, feels no remorse,
pretends it's ice armour and – ridiculous! – that he chose
it for glamour. Not even his pinkie can move.

Sounds like trauma to me. In the winter
of sixty-three, the ground froze for a hundred and thirty
days, and no graves could be dug. I heard of a heron
which, landed to fish, while the stream turned sluggish,
riffles thickened to shackles, to hold
her fast, live carrion. Then came the foxes.

Relic

The mammoth Lybua drowned in a mudhole during a late
Pleistocene ice age. She was found in 2006, now she travels
world-wide in luxury, form-fitting foam – her soul
more body than not and very well cushioned.

Don't you love a good fact, how it saves you
from feeling – for forty-two thousand years and counting –
the terror of sinking, that horrible gurgling?

Chronic Fatigue

The Tired Plant
won't grow for those
without patience. I have

what it takes, bow down
with the weight
of blossoms so luscious

they deserve to be
laid, not dropped,
on the baize-

green lawn, with a
croupier's care – she
never despairs,

no matter the odds:
'Ladies and gents, please
place your bets.'

Desolation

A charred landscape from the school of Siena,
saint in the foreground, stuck on a path
blocked by a lion. The painter's town
in the distance has nothing to teach them,
they are its centre: violence, devastation
and, much more hazardous, hope.

Ice Mummy

So easily done: hunting, you slip on a rock,
hit your head, drop bow and arrows, to drown
in a pool inches deep. Game over.

Not quite. Thick ice remembers
each detail of where, how you fell,
what you were hunting, for later inspection.

A glacier discovery: he twitches alive,
claims it was murder, outlines his plans,
chatty, now that the weather's warmer.

The Long Crawl up Humanity's Beach

'Strange sea-creature that I have become, seeing light
through ice cataracts, legs wasted, amphibious, drawing in air
like knives to my proto-gills, lips blue, fingers wrinkled, unable
to understand the shouts and gestures of people
who run down the sand towards me, bearing colourful towels,
flasks, reassurance. They seem pleased to see me…
I look up, blunt-eyed, through a freezing headache.

Warm me too quickly, I'm dead. Leave me cold
beneath a tarpaulin because now is the time
of most danger, while life is returning.'

Ear, Nose and Throat

Aged four, Rob and I –both prone to catarrh –
went for tonsil- and adenoidectomies. Across cots, we shared

Alphabet Sweets, so decided to marry but each faced the knife
alone. We woke to jelly, ice cream, blancmange: the wedding

feast of our Promised Land. Our tonsils were bloom-covered grapes,
so heavy with juice that the surgeons slung them on poles,

and carried them, swinging, to be trodden to must
elsewhere. First husband, I miss you. All the way home on the bus,

I went round telling passengers what I'd lost, showing
the cave of my echoing mouth, the scroll of my testament tongue

and, at its root, an absence. Some adults smiled, amused
but I insisted, moved even closer, opening wide.

Grottarossa Mummy

Palazzo Massimo, Rome

Wearing my rucksack like an aqualung, I descend
to the Basement of Jewels and Preciousness to view
its chief treasure: the mummified girl, thirteen years and nine
centuries old in a glass coffin. I share my air supply with her
and the child confides that, from her sky faces stare
down at her then, indifferent as clouds or gods move on,
and do I know where dolly went, she must be so lonely?

She's in a separate case, out of reach, so
thoughtless! Conqueror of time and space, I break
the glass, place the toy back in the crook of her arm.
She sits up, shows me that dolly's hips, knees, elbows
still move – she's waving hello! – then confides
that one time a dog pressed its nose, cold, to the back
of her leg and that changed everything.

III RECOVERY

The infant has a prolonged sense of the uncanny, as he dwells with a spirit of place the creation of which is not indentifiable.

CHRISTOPHER BOLLAS
The Shadow of the Object

Awake

What woke me was not a kiss
but an injection. Bewitched
by my brain waves, I fell ill
in a genteel herbaceous border.
Now it's a thicket of thorns.

How will I ever find
my old life? Give
up. Learn to cultivate
shade, rejoice in mosses.

Flowers of the Wayside and Meadow

(B. James, Bryn Villa, Dec 1928)

I'm learning the grasses with my dead Dacu
from his textbook. First page, he's keen:
Sweet Vernal Grass puts the sugars in hay.
He ticks Sheep's Fescue, but neglects

the fashion-parade crescendo
through Pinks, Poppies, Spurges,
not noting – as I do now – that an Orchid's
two tubers in Welsh are called 'Adam and Eve'.

Eve sinks in water but, hey, Adam floats…
He knows that Nettle's a 'weapon' and that Horse-tail
(whetting rushes) are full of silica, used to sharpen
arrows, this written only a decade after

the battle of Ypres, in which he was wounded.
No wonder he leaves me when humble Bracken's
rhizomes are described 'like soldiers in dugouts'.
I continue alone to the difficult lichens.

A Litter Herbal

On your left is the nest
of a secret drinker: a collection of glass
like a box of jewels.
Tourmaline, garnets shine
through the scrub. No matter

how often the obsessive litter
picker plunders the bower, overnight
bottles – perfect as eggs – and fragrant
with malt reappear,
so resilient
is pain and the instinct

to hide it. We could keep watch,
to observe this creature
and approach with advice…
No. Anguish deserves
its own privacy.

Late Blackberries

Where was I during the glut? I missed
the first sweetness, alluring and glossy

black as a dormouse's eye, when pickings
were easy. A decade lost being ill tastes

bitter. Not for me a harvest
still young and maggot-free… No

matter, I'm here for the final
sugar-rush, as fruit flush to bruises.

I hunt under leaves for berries
hard as bluebottle eyes, sucked dry

by moths and false wasps. The brambles
scratch lines of bright rubies inside my thigh:

the sun's a tattooist in blackthorn's pores
needling new patterns in blood-red haws.

On Stopping the Anti-Depressants

I thought I was dead –
my tears were shards
of glass scattered round
to keep the unwary
from my waste ground.

Now, I'm a statue that moved:
a rare plant has flowered
after fifteen years, in my eyes
grow buds, then blossoms
of brine, then a fountain
of flowers falling in sprays
like fuchsia, known in the Irish
as *deora dé*, God's tears.
While I cry, he weeps me. Come
closer now darlings, bathe in this pool,
while you can, of suffering shed
overflowing and cool.

Three Ways into Water

As the kid dared me: 'Dive straight in and swim
for your life!' That's braving the surface's axe, to emerge
a severed Tudor head in lace ruff, still wearing
drop-pearl earrings and, post-execution, gasping:
'It's lovely in, if you can bear it!'

I take my pain slowly, striptease in reverse:
feet flinch as I unroll water's inhuman
socks to my knees and then – sharp intake of breath –
pull icy girdle to groin, over nipples, armpits and nape
then there's nothing to lose till the ice-cream ache
in sinuses, then total submersion, being scalped.

I push my face right past the cascade,
static thrums
on my skull. Like Flammarion's monk,
I've thrust my head
through sky's skin, can see how my brain
is dazzled
by stars' wheels and zigzags,
spelling delight,
which is the opposite of pain.

The Beat

I am that untimely tree, out of sync
with seasons, seeking the beat –
called the One – for healing. I'm always too soon

or right after. Just off. I'm still part
(however peripheral) of the band, me
with my triangle, waiting and counting

through the cacophony. We're all playing badly –
two – one – and I'm in! We end up together,
look round in surprise and burst out laughing.

Riverlarking
(for Clare Shaw)

I've lain in a chilling Yorkshire stream
for decades, allowing eddies and pools
to dream me. My body's a shorthand:
the legs up to torso a Y, *disjecta membra*
of woman, the water leaving impossible
questions unanswered, but never entirely.
I'm part of a sentence, a meme.

Down come her salvaging fist through riffles,
breaking the surface, like God's blessing hand,
from a cloud, to change all rules, pulling me through
so my shoulder-blades warm on her palm. I am found.

FIRST RAIN IN PARADISE

(Diptych in *World Chronicle*, German, *c.* 1400–1410)

Previous

Of before, I can't speak, except to say
we were trapped in the tapestry, each thread
went through us: the chainmail

fishscales strobing in rivers, the stag
in his musk but – already – the fortified wall
and hoopoe primed to witness our fall.

Shame

Yes, I held the knife,
but the snake with a cyborg face,
all rage and reason,
made me do it and yes, we burned
down the barn – all those tortoises
cooked in their shells, not to mention

the matted cats. We lit
blackthorn hedges to drifting smoke:
foot-and-mouth funeral pyres

but nobody came, so we hid
from the first fat drops, then it pelted
down, zigzagging the hills

out of shape, smudging our groins
like an artist's thumb. Ashamed, we fled.
Anything, anything not to be seen.

Kidnapped

'What japes we had in the 1980s! One night,
out of term, I was stripped naked tied up, bundled
into a car, blindfolded. "Be charming,"

I thought to myself. They dumped me, alone
high on the pitch-black, freezing moors.
There was a pub, but nobody answered.

Then they came back, switched to full beam,
started revving. So funny! I took it all in good part.'
His smile's the entrance to a mine shaft.

Floods

After the hissing pillars of rain
held up in glass temples by intemperate gales
collapsed into rubble, the falling begins:

paths become runnels, carrying twig
bouquets, wooing smaller mercury streams
from guttering, spilling down gullies,

into drains that can't swallow, making the road
a ford, and the A32 a steel-
sheeted rink of aquaplane.

The floodplains' scrying glass takes days
to fill with run-off. Allotments are covered
in foil tarpaulins, seeds rot, but under

Seaport's waterlogged car park the arrow
shows *This Way Out*. Where now
are the two who spent their days playing cards

in the bus stop? Their tent in the woods
is untenable. Floodwater rolls its eyes at the sky
as the moribund do, learning to die.

Expulsion

To blackbirds, the ancient privilege
of bringing down day, calling alarm: 'Leave
feeders! Huddle together in roosts!

Hide!' Photon by photon Earth turns
away from her source. The kingfisher sky's
flayed bloody. Dark's coming. An owl
descends – clutching stars and dismay
in her talons. Stubborn as ever, I choose to stay.

Ornithology

The Wood Thrush sings a duet
all by itself, using two separate
voices, while the Whip-Bird's one cry – two creatures,
nothing between them, though you know the fiction,
standing on Point Sublime to listen:

One. Are we
one? We are…
one.

An Explanation of Doily
(for Adam Zagajewski)

You asked me last summer: 'What is a doily?'
Sometimes, at lunch, I walk on the beach.
Today I was coatless. A storm cloud threatened,
dark as a spaceship. Should it pour,
a sister ship down in the water
would throw up grappling nets to the surface,
rain rise to soak me. Behind a sandbank,
waves touched the shore, no more than a shimmer.

Less rare than its cousin, the antimacassar,
a doily's placed between sweet thing and china.
Both survive where vicars arrive
for tea, are given thin cup and saucer
Instead of a mug. If your cake's so rich
that it's leaking syrup, you'll need a doily.
Held up, its paper's the filigree
of snowflake, or fingers looked through in fear.

The shower holds off. My shoe's a doily.
Without it, where would I be on these shells
that crunch underfoot, like contact lenses,
as I walk, a mermaid, on razor-torn feet
back to my husband in his human dwelling?

Someone is pulling a blue toy trawler
along the horizon to port, so smoothly
it looks realistic. Sea's partly doily.
Surfers ride its lace to their downfall,
after all, we're nothing but froth.

Like a carpet salesman, the indolent tide
flops a wave over, showing samples: 'Madam,
this one is durable, has a fringe.' Under
its breath the sea sighs, 'Has it come
to this? Must everything always end in…doily?'

It must. Broad afternoon. The rain-cloud barges
have passed and here's a cumulonimbus parade
of imperial busts, the Roman rulers
in historical order which, I think, would please you.
Their vapour curls and noble foreheads
are lit up in lilac because they're invading
the west. Next come the philosophers and, last of all,
the poets. Pulleys draw them delicately on.
Here comes Lucretius, then Ovid, then Horace
in lines, saying relentlessly, 'Doily', 'Doily',
till stars take over and do the same.

NOTES & ACKNOWLEDGEMENTS

'**Principalities, Dominions**': The quotation at the end is from A.D. Imms, *Insect Natural History* (The New Naturalist series, Collins, 1947), p.127. The poem was commissioned by the Learned Society of Wales. An earlier version appeared in *Prac Crit* http://www.praccrit.com/contributor/gwyneth-lewis/.

'**Tragedy**': Clytemnestra plots her revenge against her husband, Agamemnon, who sacrificed their daughter, Iphigenia, in order to reach Troy. My play *Clytemnestra* was commissioned and performed by Cardiff's Sherman Cymru in 2012. This poem draws on the actual stage manager's notes for the run. The play's available as a free pdf on my website www.gwynethlewis.com.

'**Another Day Ill in Bed**': The poem is translated from my own Welsh, 'Diwrnod Arall yn Dost yn y Gwely'. It and 'A Litter Herbal', 'Awake', 'Fatigue', '*Flowers of the Wayside and Meadow*', 'Late Blackberries', 'On Stopping the Anti-Depressants', 'The Beat' and 'Will I?' were part of *Cultural Cwtsh*, an Arts Council of Wales project commissioning artists to support the healthcare workforce in Wales. It enabled me to start working again after a period of ill health and I'm very grateful both for the project's ethos and its support during the pandemic. My work and that of the other artists who took part can be seen at https://culturalcwtsh.wales/bittersweet-herbal.

'Red Waistcoat' ('Y Wasgod Goch') is the title of a Welsh folk song about death.

'Persephone at CERN' and 'Earrings from the Anti-Matter Factory' were commissioned by the Conseil Européen pour la Recherche Nucléaire in Geneva.

'Under' was commissioned by BBC Radio 4's *Today* programme in response to the Gleision mining disaster of 2011.

'Rogue Female' draws on Geoffrey Household's 1939 cult thriller *Rogue Male*, in which a failed assassin goes to ground to confront his pursuer.

Other poems have appeared in *The Aftershock Review*, *Bad Lilies*, *The Dark Horse*, *PN Review*, *Poetry*, Poetry London, *Poetry Wales*, *Prac Crit*, *Scintilla* and *The Yale Review*.

The epigraph is from 'Do Not Be Ashamed' by Wendell Berry from his *Collected Poems: 1957–1982* (North Point Press, Berkeley, CA, 1984).

I'm extremely grateful to the Royal Literary Fund and the Society of Authors' Contingency Fund for financial support during a time of difficulty.

Clare Shaw kept me encouraging company while I was revising many of these poems and asked the right questions. Isobel Armstrong took time and trouble to read the whole manuscript and her insights and generosity have made this a better book. Poet and scholar Richard Greene read the manuscript at a key point and gave me the benefit of his acute critical eye. I'm fortunate to have such readers.

My debt to everyone at Bloodaxe is, as ever, profound. Their commitment to the long and demanding work of publishing and promoting contemporary poetry is legendary and I thank them for their stamina and integrity. Along with Neil Astley and Christine Macgregor, I would like to thank Suzanne Fairless-Aitken, Pete Hebden, Rebecca Hodkinson, Bethan Jones and Jean Smith, as well as Pamela Robertson-Pearce for her contribution.

Leighton, my husband, has seen me through everything.

EU DECLARATION OF GPSR CONFORMITY

Books published by Bloodaxe Books are identified by the EAN/ISBN printed above our address on the copyright page and manufactured by the printer whose address is noted below. This declaration of conformity is issued under the sole responsibility of the publisher, the object of declaration being each individual book produced in conformity with the relevant EU harmonisation legislation with no known hazards or warnings, and is made on behalf of Bloodaxe Books Ltd on 27 March 2025 by Neil Astley, Managing Director, editor@bloodaxebooks.com.

No part of this book may be used or reproduced in any manner for the purpose of training artificial intelligence technologies or systems. The publisher expressly reserves *First Rain in Paradise* from the text and data mining exception in accordance with European Parliament Directive (EU) 2019/790.